THE TUNNEL

Contents

Frankenbike

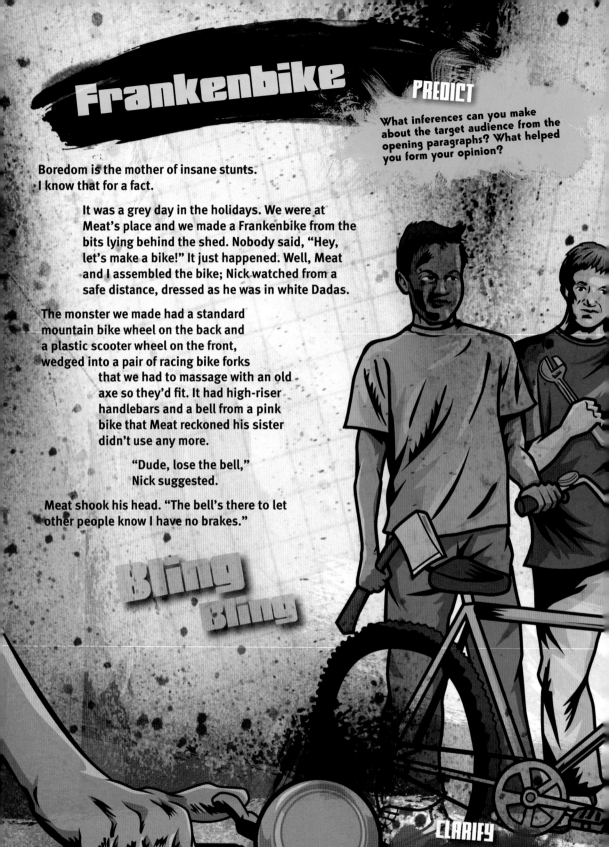

PREDICT

What inferences can you make about the target audience from the opening paragraphs? What helped you form your opinion?

Boredom is the mother of insane stunts. I know that for a fact.

It was a grey day in the holidays. We were at Meat's place and we made a Frankenbike from the bits lying behind the shed. Nobody said, "Hey, let's make a bike!" It just happened. Well, Meat and I assembled the bike; Nick watched from a safe distance, dressed as he was in white Dadas.

The monster we made had a standard mountain bike wheel on the back and a plastic scooter wheel on the front, wedged into a pair of racing bike forks that we had to massage with an old axe so they'd fit. It had high-riser handlebars and a bell from a pink bike that Meat reckoned his sister didn't use any more.

"Dude, lose the bell," Nick suggested.

Meat shook his head. "The bell's there to let other people know I have no brakes."

Bling Bling

CLARIFY

a permanent endo
phat motorbike noises
hacked a U-turn

2

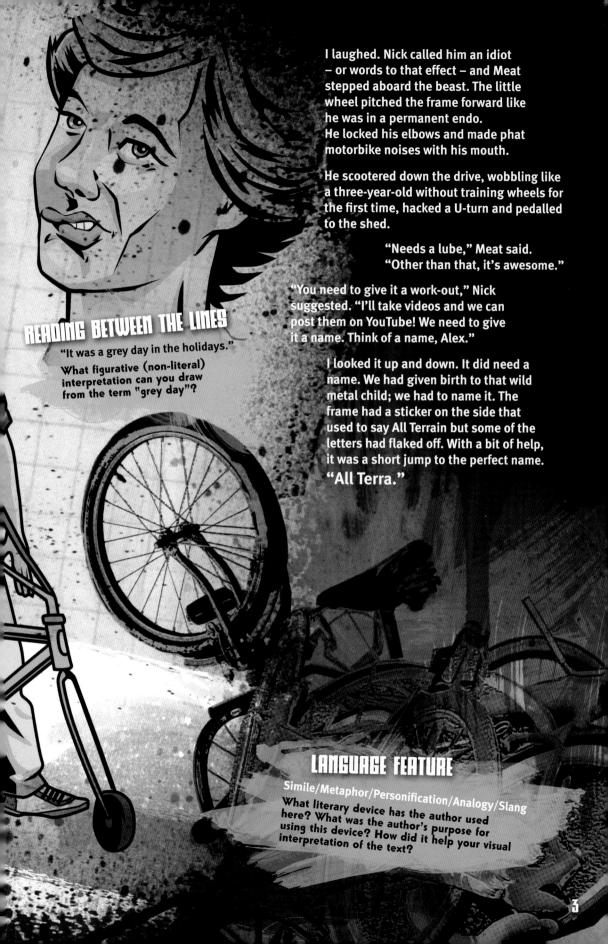

I laughed. Nick called him an idiot – or words to that effect – and Meat stepped aboard the beast. The little wheel pitched the frame forward like he was in a permanent endo. He locked his elbows and made phat motorbike noises with his mouth.

He scootered down the drive, wobbling like a three-year-old without training wheels for the first time, hacked a U-turn and pedalled to the shed.

"Needs a lube," Meat said. "Other than that, it's awesome."

"You need to give it a work-out," Nick suggested. "I'll take videos and we can post them on YouTube! We need to give it a name. Think of a name, Alex."

I looked it up and down. It did need a name. We had given birth to that wild metal child; we had to name it. The frame had a sticker on the side that used to say All Terrain but some of the letters had flaked off. With a bit of help, it was a short jump to the perfect name.

"All Terra."

READING BETWEEN THE LINES

"It was a grey day in the holidays."

What figurative (non-literal) interpretation can you draw from the term "grey day"?

LANGUAGE FEATURE

Simile/Metaphor/Personification/Analogy/Slang

What literary device has the author used here? What was the author's purpose for using this device? How did it help your visual interpretation of the text?

Meat and I took turns riding All Terra up the drive, onto the footpath and up and down the gutters while Nick took videos on his phone.

We crowded around him and watched the replays, but the only bit that made us laugh was when Meat lost control and rammed the power pole.

"I have a challenge for you," Nick said.

Meat crossed his arms. "Bring it on."

"Madigan Street."

Meat threw back his head and laughed.

Madigan Street – the whole extreme downhill kilometre of it.

ANALYSE

Why do you think Meat responds to the challenge from Nick even when there is danger involved?

...bring it on

OPINION

Do you think the author has stereotyped Meat? Why/why not?

PERSONAL RESPONSE

What connections can you make to being challenged to do something risky?

Stunt

"You're mad," I whispered.

Meat chuckled. "I know that."

He was on the footpath, perched on the very top of the hill. Madigan Street fell away below him, empty of traffic except for Nick, who was jogging his way to the bottom.

Madigan Street has a reputation.

Tamara Kennedy spent a whole maths lesson telling me stories about her street. She said it killed trucks – gave them heart attacks as they hauled their loads up its sheer face. She said if a car hit the bottom of the hill fast enough, it would scrape on the road and sparks would fly. I've seen the deep grooves in the tar way down there. I believe her stories.

CLARIFY
sheer face
maximum velocity
engine gunning
catapulted

Nick waved. He held his phone in front of him.

Meat looked pale. I could hear him breathing.

"You don't have to do this," I said.

"I know that. I'll be fine."

"Why don't you start halfway down?"

He frowned. "If I'm going to do it, it's going to be memorable. I'll either make it and have the video to prove it or I won't make it and I'll have the video and the scars to prove that."

Nick was yelling, "Come on! My phone memory is nearly full!"

Meat took a breath, kicked off and raced away.

"Whoooooooohoooooo!"

AUTHOR PURPOSE

Why do you think the author introduced Tamara's story about Madigan Street at this point?

CHARACTER ANALYSIS

What inferences can you make about the narrator (Alex) based on the way he talks to Meat about the challenge?

He launched off a gutter and took a line down the centre of the road.

I watched him and I ran.

All Terra seemed stable and under control for the first half of the hill. I reckon Meat was at maximum velocity when the speed wobbles hit. His legs shot out for balance but the wobbles only got worse. He stomped his feet onto the road and the soles of his runners screamed, but the bike didn't seem to slow. The wobbles eased, but Meat kept his shoes hard on the tar.

I know about friction. You can only use your feet as brakes for a certain amount of time until...

Meat swore and lifted his feet just as a black sports car crested the hill behind Nick, engine gunning.

Meat swerved, lost control, hit the gutter and somehow made it back onto the footpath.

If I hadn't seen the video of Meat's final stack a hundred times, I wouldn't have believed it was possible.

He wasn't on the footpath for long. Two zigs and one zag later, All Terra's front wheel hit the metal barrier that stopped cars from driving into the creek at the bottom of the hill. It was like someone had pressed the ejector seat button. Meat was catapulted over the handlebars and over the rail – a rolling tangle of limbs, crashing through branches and disappearing from sight.

LANGUAGE FEATURE

Simile/Metaphor/Personification/Analogy/Slang
What literary device has the author used here?
What was his purpose for using this device?
How did it help your understanding?

Tunnel

The car roared past, oblivious.

Nick was still filming, swearing and calling out to Meat, when I finally made it to the crashed bike.

As the car crested the hill and the noise of its engine faded, I heard laughter from below.

"Meat?"

More laughter.

"You okay?"

"Yep," he said.

"WHOOOOOOHOOOOO!"

Nick and I looked at each other and blew sighs of relief.

"Hope you got that on the phone," Meat called up. "That was classic!"

"Got it," Nick said. "Come up and check it out."

"The only moving I'm doing for the next ten minutes is shaking," said Meat.

I stepped over the rail. "Come on," I called to Nick.

"I'm not going down there," Nick said. He grabbed the front of his white jacket and frowned at me.

"Don't be a wuss," I growled.

I picked my way down to where Meat sat on a pile of broken reeds. He was smiling and shaking his head.

"Sure you're okay?"

"Fine," he said. "Check this out."

He pointed to where the creek flowed under the road. There wasn't a bridge as such, just a pipe as tall as me.

CLARIFY

oblivious
crested
rank dribble

AUTHOR PURPOSE

What strategies has the author used to target his audience directly?

"Whooooohoooo!" Meat yelled, and it echoed down the pipe. It went on forever. A semi-fossilised shopping trolley lay upturned in the tunnel's open mouth, its ribs covered in chip packets and burger wrappers. A rank dribble of rusty water leaked from the base of the pipe. The concrete around the entrance was covered in graffiti tags, mostly featuring the name Casper over and over again, but there were some stick figures being rude and a lopsided picture of a skull.

"Looks like All Terra survived," Nick shouted from up on the road. "Little buckle in the front wheel but, other than that, it's fine."

"Bring it down," Meat yelled back.

Silence.

"He doesn't want to get dirty," I said.

"Don't worry about your clothes," Meat yelled. "Come down. We've found a tunnel."

"I've seen the tunnel."

"Have you seen up the tunnel?"

"It just goes under the road."

Meat was on his feet now so we stepped past the shopping trolley and into the throat of the pipe.

SETTING
How effectively has the author developed the mood and atmosphere of the setting? What elements helped evoke a mental image of the scene?

BEYOND THE TEXT
Compare the strategies used to target the audience in *The Tunnel* to the strategies used to target young people in advertising. What are the similarities?

Into the Dark

Ten metres in, it became obvious that the pipe went further than the other side of the road. The darkness and echoey silence came out to greet us. It rode on a cool, damp breeze that smelled faintly of rotting flesh. I don't mind admitting that my heart was banging hard and, if Meat hadn't been there, I would have bolted back into the light.

Meat strode on confidently for another five steps then stopped. He shouted. It made me jump.

There was a loud metal-on-metal crash as something collided with the shopping trolley back at the tunnel entrance. It made me cover my ears.

"Here's your bike," Nick shouted. He was a silhouette at the entrance, busily wiping something off his precious jacket.

He walked to where Meat and I were frozen on the edge of the dark and started beat-boxing with the echo. He's not the best beat-boxer on the planet, but it did sound wicked in the tunnel. Meat started grooving, slapping the roof above his head and walking deeper into the abyss. I could see the reflectors on his runners and then he was gone, swallowed by the blackness.

"Meat?"

Nick stopped.

Eventually, Meat's voice came back to us. "Come on. Grab the bike. We've got to check this out."

"We haven't got a torch," Nick said. "We need a torch. Come on, let's go. I have to get changed. We can bring a torch back. The bike will be okay there. Nobody will steal it."

QUESTION

Do you think Meat and Alex are good friends to Nick? Why/why not?

BEYOND THE TEXT

What does friendship mean to you? What qualities should a good friendship have?

...swallowed

CHARACTER ANALYSIS

What inferences can you make about Nick and how he is perceived through the eyes of his friends?

"I'm not worried about it being pinched," Meat said, coming back far enough for us to see him. "I want to ride."

"In the dark?" Nick said.

"We can use your phone for light," I suggested.

"Yesssss," Meat said. "Let's do this. Let's see where it ends."

"It stinks in here," Nick said. He took a can of deodorant from his jacket and sprayed the tunnel. "I've got one of those head lamp things at home. It's as bright as."

"Dude! What's with the deo? You won't get dirty in here," I said. "It's all concrete and stuff."

I jogged back to the entrance and untangled All Terra from the trolley where Nick had dumped it. I wheeled it back to Meat and he patted the seat.

"Good beast," he said. "No bucking me off in here or this tunnel will be your grave."

I held the frame as he stepped aboard.

"Phone," Meat demanded.

Nick breathed an exasperated sigh and handed Meat his phone. "If you bust it, you owe me seven hundred dollars, right?"

"Whatever," Meat said.

READING BETWEEN THE LINES

What effect do you think Meat and Alex's ridicule has on Nick?

by the blackness

Nick Goes Down

The feeble light from the screen didn't exactly fill the tunnel, but my eyes adjusted. Meat rode through the thin track of water in the bottom. Nick and I wide-legged it to straddle the creek and stumble-jogged along behind to keep up. My heart was still doing its own beat-box thing, but I had a smile on my face. This was the sort of thing holidays were meant for.

We were in the middle of an adventure.

The tunnel curved gently to the right and, within a minute, the glow from the entrance disappeared and the phone was all we had.

Nick slipped. I heard the dull thud of limbs hitting concrete and a tiny splash. He swore.

I laughed. I couldn't see a thing, but I knew what had happened. "You okay?"

He swore again, louder this time, and Meat stopped.

"What?"

"Nick's had a bit of a fall."

Meat backed the bike up and shone the phone on Nick. His white Dadas now had a greenish-brown bum. He wiped at the slimy mess, but only managed to spread it further.

Meat chuckled.

"Give me my phone," Nick grumbled.

"Why?"

"Just give it to me," he shouted. "I'm going home."

CLARIFY

straddle
natural conclusion

AUTHOR PURPOSE

Why do you think the author focused on the way Meat and Alex ridiculed Nick? What message is the author conveying to the reader here?

BEYOND THE TEXT

What connections can you make to being ridiculed? Does ridicule have a lasting effect on people? Why/why not?

"Come on," Meat said. "We're not at the end yet."

"Do you know how much these Dadas cost?" Nick bellowed. "Three hundred bucks!"

"Yeah well, they're dirty now," I said. "Going home's not going to make them any cleaner."

"True," Meat agreed. "Might as well see it through to its natural conclusion."

"You guys owe me a new pair of pants."

"Riiiiight," Meat said. "Whatever you reckon."

"It's only drain slime," I said. "It'll wash off."

"Phone!" Nick demanded.

"Come on, Nick. Don't be such a..."

"Look!" I interrupted. With the phone directed at Nick, the tunnel ahead glowed with a light of its own. "We're nearly there."

CHARACTER ANALYSIS

What inferences can you make about Nick based on his comments about the cost of his Dadas?

...the glow
from the entrance
disappeared

Dead Things

Meat gave Nick his phone and started pedalling towards the glow. I couldn't see a thing on the ground in front of me, but I jogged on behind Meat and All Terra, each step a little leap of faith. The light had travelled a long way – I jogged for about two hundred metres before we found the source, but it wasn't the end of the tunnel.

The pipe opened into a chamber illuminated from above by the grating in a roadside drain.

CLARIFY

stalactites
gagged

Roots hung from the ceiling like stalactites. The floor of the room was covered in crushed cans and plastic bottles. A metal ladder was bolted against the wall below the grating. It was good to see the light of day, even though it was three metres over our heads.

"Oh, man, what stinks?" Nick said. He'd followed us anyway.

"Wasn't me," I said, but I smelled it, too. **The pong of death again, only this time it was right in my nostrils.**

Meat was off the bike and toeing at a hairy ball of something below the drain grating. "Here," he said. "I think it's a cat."

Nick gagged. He whipped his can of deodorant out and gave the cat carcass a good spray. Now the room stank of dead cat and deodorant.

"How do we get out?" Nick asked.

INFERENCE

What inferences can you make about the author's reason for introducing the incident with the dead cat and the deodorant?

I couldn't see a thing...

Meat climbed the ladder and pushed at the manhole cover above his head. It didn't budge. "Not that way."

"Even if we could lift it, we couldn't get All Terra out," I said.

"Then we go out the way we came," Nick said.

Meat dropped onto the layer of rubbish. "We could. That's always an option. But we're not at the end of the tunnel yet."

"Check this out," Nick said. He poked at the rubbish with his toe. It was a used syringe with the needle still attached.

"There's another one," Meat said, and I spotted a third when I bent to collect a tennis ball from the mess.

"Let's get out of here," I said.

Meat climbed aboard All Terra and pointed it in the direction of the unexplored tunnel. He looked at Nick. "Coming?"

Nick's shoulders dropped and he turned to face the tunnel we'd come through.

"You can hold the phone," Meat said. "You can go at the front."

"Why? So any crocodiles in the sewer get me first?"

Meat smiled. "That's the general idea."

Nick called him an idiot – or words to that effect – then crunched over the rubbish and into the new tunnel. Meat and I triumphantly punched fists behind his back.

It wasn't over yet.

INFERENCE

What inferences can you make about the dangers presented by the finding of the syringes?

16

PLOT

"It wasn't over yet."

What implications does this statement have for the plot and why has the author used it?

OPINION

Do you think friends should look out for one another? Why/why not?

Treasure

Chambers, drains and rubbish became more common as we ventured deeper into the pipe. Seeing the daylight every couple of hundred metres made the darkness between seem less threatening.

Each new pile of rubbish offered treasures as well as disgusting stuff. I made quite a collection of tennis balls. Meat climbed ladders and tested the manholes, but they were all too heavy. He peered out the gutter gratings and relayed what he could see.

"We're in Barkley Street!" he yelled. "I can see the letterbox next door to my dad's place. We're nearly home!"

But, in reality, we were a long way from his home. Unless we found a way out ahead, we'd have to backtrack to where the adventure started – all the way back to Madigan Street.

RESEARCH

What real-life stories can you find in media such as TV and newspapers about people stuck in stormwater drains? What were the real outcomes in these stories?

18

At the next chamber, the pipe changed. The tunnel leading out was smaller than the one we'd arrived through. The idea of having to bend down while we walked made my guts tighten.

VISUAL FEATURES
What underlying message does the visual image convey about the situation the boys are in? What parallels can you draw?

For the first time, I felt like there wouldn't be another end – that the pipes would just keep getting smaller until we got stuck.

Meat didn't have to bend. Sitting atop All Terra, he was a comfortable fit in the new pipe.

His eyes were wide. "Now it's getting interesting."

"Nope," said Nick flatly. "Now it's time to turn back."

"It's not a dead end," Meat said.

"No, but it will be soon enough," I said.

"Come on," Meat protested. "If the pipe gets any smaller than this, we turn around and go back. Promise."

ISSUES
What, in your view, are the main issues in this book? How do you think the boys should respond to these?

...it's time to turn back

19

Nick took the lead again and I walked right behind him — so close that I kicked him in the heel. Twice.

"Ow! Watch what you're doing, Alex."

"Sorry."

"What's the matter with you? Give me some room."

What *was* the matter with me? The fun was gone.

Suddenly, the adventure wasn't an adventure any more.

You take the fun away and it turns into a sort of punishment, a torture. Meat had seemed like the big brave explorer until the fun went. Now he looked like an idiot bossing us around and bent on self-destruction. I didn't want to be part of that. I was ready for it to be over, but I knew it would take almost as long to get out as it had to get in.

I laughed when we burst into another chamber and the light from the drain above revealed three small pipes. They were big enough to crawl through and they entered at shoulder height. This was the end. I knew we'd have to turn around. I found another tennis ball and a cigarette lighter that sparked but wouldn't hold a flame. I stuffed it in my bulging pocket anyway.

PERSONAL RESPONSE

How would you respond if you were in Alex's situation?

"Jackpot!" Nick hollered. "Check it out!"

He'd found a leather purse. It was misshapen, as if it had been wet and then dried, but when he unzipped it we all sucked in our breath.

It was stuffed with cash. Two hundred and sixty-five dollars, to be exact. There were credit cards, store cards and a driver's licence.

"Gail Edwards," Nick read. "She lives on Claremont Drive. Don't know her."

"Give us a look," Meat said. He took the licence and studied the picture, then shook his head. He handed it to me.

"She looks a bit like that chick who works in the video shop."

"A bit," Nick agreed, and his phone beeped.

"Message?" Meat asked.

I heard Nick swallow. "Low battery."

"You're joking," I said.

He shook his head solemnly.

In the brief silence that followed, we heard music. At least, it sounded like music – faint and buried in white noise, as if the radio wasn't quite tuned in. We had time to look at each other, puzzled, before the small pipe above Nick spewed water onto his jacket.

READING BETWEEN THE LINES

"Suddenly, the adventure wasn't an adventure any more. You take the fun away and it turns into a sort of punishment."

What inferences can you make about how Alex feels about the tunnel now and how his behaviour might change?

21

An Instant River

"What the...?"

"Somebody flushed their toilet,"
Meat said with a nasty chuckle.

The two other pipes and the drain
above us began dripping.

"It's not the sewer,"
I said. "It's stormwater."

Meat swore, grabbed All Terra and shoved it
back in the direction we'd come from.

I shoved Nick after him. "Go!" I screamed.

"What?"

"It's raining!"

PLOT

Has the plot been convincing/
unconvincing in your opinion?
How do you think the story
will conclude?

CHARACTER ANALYSIS

Summarise what you know about the characters, using evidence from the text and the inferences you have made.

Evidence from the Text

Inferential Information

Nick   Meat   Alex

How credible/incredible were the characters in your opinion?

Nick's phone beeped like a dying bird. If it
died, we'd be in total darkness. The trickle
of water beneath our feet had become a
flow. We burst into the chamber where
the pipe changed size and were instantly
soaked by the waterfall that surged in off
the road above. We ran, the current ankle-
deep and rising.

When the battery in Nick's phone finally
gave out, the darkness that swallowed us
was complete. "Noooooo!" Nick howled.
His voice echoed along the tunnel and
was eventually drowned by the sound of
rushing water.

Meat had stopped. "It's okay,
Nick," he said. His voice was
as reassuring as my mum's in
the black of a nightmare. "We
can do this. We'll be okay. We
just follow the water. One step
at a time. Let's go."

LANGUAGE FEATURE

Simile/Metaphor/Personification

What literary devices has the author
used here? What was his purpose fo
using these devices? How did it help
your understanding of the text?

But the darkness was so total that we became
disoriented after two or three steps. Nick was
whimpering in front of me, Meat breathing hard
behind. Rubbish floating in the water bumped at my
calves and I thought I felt the dead cat. I screamed
before I could stop myself.

"Let me in front," Meat yelled. "You guys can hang on
to the back."

Idea. I fished the cigarette lighter from my pocket and
sparked it. It lit up the tunnel.

"Whoah!" Meat shouted. "Do it again. Again!
Alex, you're a genius."

I gave the lighter to Meat and he used it to crack holes
in the darkness between the chambers. We were on
the long last leg of the tunnel, with the water pushing
at my thighs, when the idea really came alight.

IMAGERY

"To crack holes in the darkness."

How does the textual imagery help you to interpret the scene visually?

"Deodorant!"

Nick reluctantly parted with his can and Meat used it like a flame-thrower, filling the tunnel with light, rolling forward in the dark, then setting the stink alight again. It was Nick's idea to spray a patch on the wall of the pipe. Spray a patch, light it up, and the concrete burned like a medieval torch for half a minute.

Suddenly, Meat swore. "I dropped the lighter."

Nick called him an idiot – or words to that effect – but by then I could see daylight. The rain had never felt so good on my face.

...like a medieval torch

VISUAL FEATURES

What effect do the visual images and design have on you? How do these features influence your response to the story?

The Legend Lives On

Nick placed the purse on the counter at the video shop. "Recognise this?" he asked the girl serving. Her nametag said Gail.

"Oh...my...goodness!" she squealed.

She said it must have fallen out of her car. Three days it had been missing, and she was only just starting to panic. She gave him a hundred bucks. What was more surprising was that he gave Meat and me thirty-three dollars and thirty-five cents each. Just when you think you know somebody, they go and mess with your head by being generous!

And All Terra? The legend lives on. It rests beside the pile of bike skeletons at Meat's place. Nick posted his video of the stack. Look it up on YouTube and prepare to be amazed. That was one insane stunt.

QUESTION GENERATE

What questions can you generate about this book?

AUTHOR PURPOSE

Why do you think the author wrote this story?

MESSAGE

What is the most important message in this book for you and why?

THINK ABOUT THE TEXT

MAKING CONNECTIONS

What connections can you make to the characters, plot, setting and themes of  ?

being scared

overcoming a difficult situation

feeling helpless

making stupid decisions

experiencing peer pressure

TEHT TO SELF

experiencing close friendships

using your initiative

dealing with emotions

doing the right thing

making discoveries

facing adversity

TEXT TO TEXT/MEDIA

Talk about texts/media you have read, listened to or seen that have similar themes and compare the treatment of theme and the differing author styles.

TEXT TO WORLD

Talk about situations in the world that might connect to elements in the story.

PLANNING A CONTEMPORARY FICTION

Contemporary fiction incorporates many different genres, such as mystery, science fiction, adventure, narrative, recount...

1   Think about what **defines** contemporary fiction

Contemporary fiction connects the reader with the complex situations and events of contemporary society. It incorporates themes and contexts that are seen as:

- A REFLECTION OF THE PAST
- A MIRROR OF THE PRESENT
- AN INDICATOR OF THE FUTURE.

2   Think about the plot

Decide on a plot that has an introduction, problems and a solution, and write them in the order of sequence.

Decide on an event to draw the reader into your story. What will the main conflict/problem be?

Climax

Build your story to a turning point. This is the most exciting/suspenseful part of the story.

Conflict

Falling Action

Rising Action

Decide on a final event that will resolve the conflict/problem and bring your story to a close.

Set the scene: who is the story about? When and where is it set?

Introduction

Resolution

Think about the sequence of events and how to present them using contemporary fiction devices, such as *flashback* and *foreshadowing*.

Flashback = showing part of the storyline out of sequence.
Foreshadowing = suggesting or indicating events before they happen.

3 Think about the characters

Explore:

- how they think, feel and act
- what motivates their behaviour
- their inner feelings, using contemporary fiction approaches, such as stream of consciousness and product-of-society typecasting.

Stream of consciousness = a description of the flow of thoughts and feelings through a character's mind as they arise.

Product-of-society typecasting = giving the characters roles that are typical of the society they were born into.

4 Decide on the setting

location

atmosphere/mood   time

Note: Contemporary fiction provides a window into current lifestyles and living conditions, which are often shaped by multimedia influences.

WRITING A CONTEMPORARY FICTION

Have you...

- made links to the society and events of your period?

- identified with recurrent contemporary themes?

- maintained a fast pace of action?

- grabbed the readers' attention and dragged them from the first page to the final page?

- been true to the context of your time frame?

- provided a window on the past or present or future?

- explored contemporary values and beliefs?

- developed characters that will stand up to in-depth analysis?

...don't forget to revisit your writing. Do you need to change, add or delete anything to improve your story?